THE OLD COUNTRY

THE OLD COUNTRY

Abraham Shulman

foreword by

Isaac Bashevis Singer

CHARLES SCRIBNER'S SONS
NEW YORK

CONTENTS

ACKNOWLEDGMENTS

Most of the photographs in this book are reprints from old files of the illustrated supplement of *The Jewish Daily Forward,* the largest Yiddish daily in the world. We wish to express our thanks to the Forward Association and to its manager, Mr. Paul Rubinstein, for their kind permission to use their materials.

Many of the photographs are by Alter Katzyzne and Menachem Kipnis. Alter Katzyzne, born in Poland in 1885, was an outstanding Yiddish writer, playwright, and poet as well as a devoted artist-photographer who traveled through hundreds of Jewish towns and villages in Eastern Europe to "immortalize" the life of the shtetl. The author is especially grateful to Sulamita Katzyzne Reale of Rome for her great efforts in preserving the work of her father, Alter Katzyzne. Menachem Kipnis, born in Poland in 1878, was one of the first collectors of Yiddish folk songs, and was himself a prominent folk singer and a well-known Yiddish writer. Like Katzyzne, he was a photographer of rare talent. Both perished during the Holocaust.

FOREWORD

Isaac Bashevis Singer

In his opening essay for *The Old Country,* which precedes this remarkable collection of photos of the shtetl, Abraham Shulman retells the story of the lost world of the Eastern European Jews. But the shtetl, which was not a physical presence only but also an idea and belief, couldn't have become totally lost. Many of its qualities live on, changed in form, but nevertheless retaining the essence of their content. The great majority of the Jews in this country are descendants of the people depicted in these photos. This book will contribute to their search for identity. It will, at least in part, answer the so-often-asked question: "Who am I?"

The photos reveal how deeply rooted Jewish life in the shtetl was which explains why the Jews who came to this country at the beginning of the century brought along a determined will not to melt away in the so called Melting Pot. The poor shtetl Jews did not come to this country to forget their history, to lose their identity, but to continue to be the People of the Book, devoted to their 4,000 year old traditions. They wanted to be good Jews and faithful citizens of their newly adopted country. Their faces tell us: We came to live and worship in freedom and dignity and not to become spiritual slaves. Those people suffered, perhaps, from many sicknesses, but amnesia wasn't one of them.

And still another thing: This book reminds us once more that it is of the highest importance that men remember the cruelties of which they are capable and the power of destruction which is man's curse. Shulman's book is a grim reminder of these ugly powers. It speaks to us in words and pictures. It shows us the victims as they lived, worked, worshipped, hoped. Their faces, their eyes, ask constantly: What have we done to deserve such pain? And what are we doing to prevent such acts from repeating themselves in the future? When modern man indulges more and more in compassion for murderers of all kinds, trying to find various excuses for their evil deeds, this book manages to tell us that the victims too should be remembered.

THE OLD COUNTRY

THE OLD COUNTRY

The several hundred photographs in this book have been chosen from a much larger number. The difficulty was not what to retain but what, regretfully, to leave out, for each of these photos is an extraordinary document of a life that has no equal in the history of human culture, a life that was absolutely unique in its form and content.

The photos were taken over a period of some sixty years, mostly between 1860 and 1920, at a time when life in the Old Country, in the so-called shtetl in Eastern Europe, was at its peak. All the photographers except for the two professionals, Alter Katzyzne and Menachem Kipnis, were amateurs moved by the richness of the subjects or carried by a subconscious desire to preserve episodes of Jewish life for posterity. The photos depict the shtetl in its various aspects—there are general views of the shtetl with its marketplace, houses, stores, stalls, and pushcarts as well as synagogues, houses of study, and ritual baths. Most of the photos, however, show the extraordinary faces of the people—the aged and the young; the Hasidim in their traditional raiment; the pious Jews on their way from the shul wearing their prayer shawls; the learners in the course of making scholarly interpretations of a Talmudic text; the refined upper-class Jews; the erudites; the wealthy; and the scholars; the humble people—the coachmen, the wood hewers, the water carriers, and the beggars; elderly

1

men indulging in the intricacies of a "political" chat; children playing around the well in the center of the market.

Despite this variety of subjects and themes, there is a prevailing mood of simplicity and innocence permeating the photos. There is a family portrait with an imposing patriarchal pair in the center, surrounded by a cluster of fantastically dressed youngsters; the figure of a whiskered man or of a matronly woman in a crinoline that makes her look as if she were swimming majestically across the photo; a destitute tailor, a shoemaker who wears no shoes. Each photo carries the marks which characterize them all—serenity, innocence. Even the photos of those who, because of their convictions or occupations should look militant and aggressive—the uniformed firemen, the group of soldiers, the revolutionaries who "swore to overthrow the tsar"— show tranquillity and, again, innocence.

This same mood permeates other elements as well: the shtetl's decor—the streets, the buildings, the marketplace, a beehive of hustle and bustle. This impression of innocence has nothing to do with our conscious or inadvertent inclination to romanticize, as one is bound to do with a vanished past; neither is it an impression formed by our awareness of the shtetl's tragic end. Looking at this collection one is conscious of traveling back in time to a world that may have existed before the discovery of the tree of knowledge. This biblical connection is very real. No wonder Rembrandt frequented the synagogues and ghetto streets of Amsterdam to catch the spirit of the Bible.

The mood of serenity, even optimism, that flows from these photos does not come from the subjects themselves, since many of them are too grim and even tragic to create such a mood. It comes, instead, from a subterranean layer, which makes this peculiar chapter of Jewish life in Eastern Europe more than just a social and cultural phenomenon.

Despite its uniqueness, this album of Jewish life in the shtetl is at the same time a document that belongs to the Family of Man. The life in the settlements, which we are used to calling the shtetl, and which was limited to a geographic area and to a specific time, nevertheless was a part of human life. What makes it stand out was the particularity of its experience.

The word *shtetl* has become a part of our vocabulary. We know that a majority of the Jewish immigrants to America came from the shtetl, that Jewish literature grew out of the shtetl. We use the word to describe a cultural and social pattern; but what is a shtetl? What did it look like? What were its essentials?

These are not easy questions to answer. In the course of time the name became an abstraction, a term that moved away from its original meaning. Linguistically the word *shtetl* is a diminutive of the word *shtot,* which means "a town," and has the same origin as the English word "state." Shtetl was thus a little town. But "a little town" is by no means a shtetl. Shtetl could mean only one thing—a little town in Eastern Europe, inhabited by Jews, either exclusively or in its majority. Even in a town where the Jews were in the minority, their area of concentration still constituted a shtetl. The population of a shtetl varied from a mere few hundred to a few thousand. In addition to and apart from the shtetl, there were still smaller settlements which had received an additional diminutive suffix: *shtetele,* meaning "little shtetl," and having no more than a few dozen people. There is a Yiddish expression which describes these little places as "not bigger than a yawn."

But the shtetl or the shtetele had to possess the basic, indispensable elements, without which it would not have been viable. First was the shul, a house of prayer. It varied in size and form; it could be an imposing brick or timber building or simply an ordinary room just large enough for the congregation of male adults (every Jew over the age of thirteen). A shul was indispensable. Second was the ritual bath which, in addition to being a place for general hygiene, made Jewish family life possible. Jewish women could not be wives to their husbands without going through a number of regulations connected with the ritual bath, for

3

according to Jewish law, the "purification" of women after menstruation could be achieved only by a ritual bath. Third was the *cheder,* a primary school for the youngest children. Depending on its size, a shtetl could also have a yeshivah, a school of higher learning.

Also required was the ritual slaughterer, because dietary laws, one of the foundations of Jewish life, called for kosher meat. As for cemeteries, only the larger shtetls could afford them. In other cases the dead had to be carried to neighboring towns. But such a cemetery had to be exclusively Jewish. Because it was a holy place, it would have been unthinkable to have a Jewish section in a general place of burial, although this practice occurred in other countries. If the shtetl was particularly small, its inhabitants had to share with another town not only the cemetery, the shul, the ritual bath, the ritual slaughterer, but even their *melamed* (teacher) for the *cheder.* In such a situation the little town was simply called a *yishuv,* meaning "settlement."

The center of the shtetl was always the marketplace, paved and having in its middle a well, or, if more modern, a pump. The water was drawn either by the inhabitants themselves or by a professional water carrier. He carried pails of water to his customers on his shoulders if the shtetl was small; otherwise, if he could afford a horse, he made his deliveries storing the water in a big barrel.

Surrounding the marketplace were the houses of the wealthier Jews. In rare cases these houses were two stories high, built of brick, usually with balconies or porches. Houses in the marketplace commonly contained stores. Some were butcher shops, groceries, hardware and soft goods stores. Others, on a relatively larger scale, carried a greater variety of goods and were, accordingly, referred to as general stores. Except for the marketplace and perhaps a main street which ran the length of the shtetl and was paved, the streets, with their shabby wooden houses, were covered with dust in dry weather and deep in mud when it rained. Men and women wore boots, not for fashion, but out of necessity.

For a very long time the only street lighting at night

was the moon, assuming, of course, that the sky was clear and the moon was in its right phase. Those who ventured out on cloudy nights or when the moon was new had to carry their own candles or lanterns.

As mentioned earlier, most synagogues were simply places of worship, built in a functional style, with sufficiently large rooms to accommodate the congregants as well as the necessary Holy Ark, which was placed against the eastern wall, in the direction of Jerusalem; the *bimah,* an elevated platform where a desk was placed for reading the Torah, was usually in the center of the room, along with the lectern for the cantor; there were simple, wooden benches for the worshipers. Very often the only ornaments embellishing this spartan interior were the Holy Scrolls of the Torah inside the Ark, written by a trained scribe on strips of parchment or vellum and sewn together to form a long roll, with each end wound on a wooden stave. Each scroll was girded with a strip of silk and robed in a richly decorated mantle. The edges of the scrolls were supported and protected by two rollers of hard wood called, like the Torah itself, *Etz Hachaim,* "the Tree of Life." The projecting handles of the rollers on both sides, or at least the upper ones, were usually made of ivory. The scrolls were often surmounted with silver crowns. The Ark was also frequently adorned with a silver crown, which symbolized the Crown of Law. In front of the Ark hung a decorative curtain with religious symbols.

At this point it should be mentioned that the size and location of a synagogue were frequently determined by the regulations and orders of the Christian clergy. A synagogue could not stand too close to a church because the Jewish prayers were sure to interfere with the Christian services. Nor could a synagogue be taller and more imposing than a church. The discrimination between man and man was extended to the houses of God. The majority of synagogues were plain, spartan, ascetic in structure, and pragmatic. But there were so many exceptions to this rule that they formed a rule of their own.

History books seldom mention the many synagogues

of stone and brick which were marvels of architecture and beauty. In 1957 the Architectural Department of the Warsaw Polytechnic in Poland published an extraordinary, almost unbelievably beautiful book, *Wooden Synagogues,* which contains several hundred photos of timber synagogues in Eastern Europe. These buildings combined the most interesting architectural forms with a gripping beauty. Some of them had second stories, beautifully carved towers, external galleries. The interiors were adorned with paintings and exquisite carvings. The Jewish artists skillfully avoided violating the commandment "thou shalt not make images" by painting and sculpting objects of religious symbolism. Their work carried the seeds for the future artists, among them Soutine and Chagall.

Some of the shuls, even the wooden ones, were built in the form of fortresses, complete with heavy gates that could be locked from the inside, which served in cases of hostile attacks and pogroms. At the time of the Ukrainian massacres in the seventeenth century, the inhabitants of Jewish settlements saved their lives in these fortresses, protected by the Holy Scrolls within and by the heavy walls and defenders on the towers without.

Despite the fact that the shtetl was usually surrounded by fields, woods, or forests, it was very rare to find trees and plants in the shtetl itself, every inch of space being exploited for more useful purposes. Usually after the Sabbath meal, the promenade was taken in fields outside the town, if there was no danger of being harassed by unfriendly neighbors. A safer walk was in the alleys of the cemetery, if there was one within reach.

The shtetl was full of animals, mostly poultry: chickens, geese, ducks; occasionally a home had a calf or a goat. Cats were the only popular house pets, often given Jewish names and spoken to in Yiddish. Dogs, because of their temper and readiness to bite, were considered non-Jewish and were seldom found in a Jewish household.

When did the shtetl originate? There is no definite answer. Legends are mixed with facts, the legends having the upper hand. It is customary to assume—assumptions being a weak substitute for facts—that there were Jewish settlements in Eastern Europe as early as the eighth and ninth centuries. Some of these settlers may have come from the south, from the lands of Kiev and Byzantium, and were reinforced (here we are on shaky ground) by the Khazars. The Khazars were a Turkish or Finnish tribe that settled in the lower Volga region after the eighth century and formed a powerful state. About 800 their king Bulan and 4,000 of his nobles accepted Judaism. The Khazar state was smashed by the Russian archduke Yaroslav in 1083, but descendants of the Khazars probably mixed with Jews of Eastern European origin. Other Jews may have arrived from the west, merchants from Bohemia and Germany. The only specific date which emerges is 905, the year when a number of Jewish traders "helped open the Eastern territories to the civilization of the West" and when they presumably received a charter. A more tangible proof of Jewish presence in Eastern Europe are Polish coins of the twelfth and thirteenth centuries, struck by Jewish mint masters and carrying Hebrew inscriptions. At the same time some villages are mentioned by such names as *Zydow, Zydowo, Sidowo,* and *Kozara,* the first three meaning "Jewish Settlement," the fourth, "Khazar Settlement."

But all this does not account for the creation of the shtetl as a unit of Jewish settlement. The shtetl probably originated in the thirteenth century, when the rulers of vast parts of Eastern European territories, devastated by the invasion of the Tatars, encouraged an immigration of merchants from the west. This brought a considerable number of Jews, mostly from Germany, into Eastern Europe for the first time. It was not only the opportunity for profits that lured the German Jews into taking "the walking stick" and moving east; they were prompted by a more pressing matter: the wave of massacres and pogroms in their German homeland, particularly at the time of the Black Death when Jews were accused of deliberately causing the epidemics. (I am using here the word "pogrom," Russian in origin, which was first used in English at the time of the anti-Jewish outbreaks in Russia in 1905; it is a word that radiates its sordid light in many historical directions.)

The Jews who arrived from Germany brought, apart from their commercial aptitudes and artisan's skills, two essential traits which became the cultural and spiritual foundation of the future Eastern European Jewish community: an unlimited devotion to religion, and the Yiddish language, which at that time was the language of the majority of the Ashkenazi Jews. (Ashkenazim was the name given to the German Jews, in contrast to the Sephardim, or the Jews from Spain.) Yiddish mixed the medieval German of the Middle Rhine with elements of Hebrew, which predominated in the religious sphere. After settling in the east, Yiddish opened widely to the influx of a new important component—the Slavic.

The history of the Jewish settlers in Poland, Lithuania, and parts of Russia can be seen in terms of geological upheavals, a history which had very brief periods of tranquillity, even prosperity, and long periods of misery; short episodes of tolerance and much longer, uninterrupted periods of discrimination and violence; accusations of "desecrating Christian Hosts" and the never-ceasing accusation of Ritual Blood, the allegation that Jews murdered Christians in order to obtain blood for Passover and other rituals. Except for two towns, where the Christian clergy succeeded in establishing closed and locked ghettos (Lwow and in the Krakow suburb of Kazimierz), the Jews lived in the shtetlech and in special sections in the cities.

It should be kept in mind that the Jews were invited, with promises of protection that were assured by charters defining their legal rights and the framework of their legal employment and freedom. These charters also regulated legal suits between Jews and non-Jews. The Jews who were invited by the rulers to develop their backward provinces found themselves in an environment of illiterate peasants, half-literate city dwellers, and faced with a church which had infused into the whole Christian population the belief that the Jews were the killers of their God. Part of the hos-

8

tility they encountered therefore had religion as its base. Other reasons for hostility came somewhat later with the emergence of native merchants and artisans, with whom the Jews were economic competitors. As if this were not enough, we must add the one element which has been at the root of anti-Semitism at all stages of Jewish history: the total lack of any real reason whatsoever, indeed the prevalence of unreason.

The year 1264 was a memorable one for the Jews in Poland, for that was the year when the king Bolesaw the Pious signed the model charter of protection. Seventy years later another Polish king, who is regarded with special sympathy in Jewish tradition, Kazimierz the Great, signed the so-called Statute of Kalish, extending the previous charter to White Russia and Little Poland. Twenty-four years later it was further extended to embrace the Jews in Lithuania. But the foundations of these nice-sounding charters were shaky. They were constantly twisted and limited by succeeding rulers and, finally in 1454, they were totally abolished.

Despite this capricious wind of tolerance, meager privilege, and tangible acts of violence, Jewish life continued, playing an important part in the economy of the Eastern European countries. During the reigns of two liberal kings, Sigismund the First and Sigismund Augustus, in the sixteenth century, conditions were relatively good. But the brief period of respite ended in a great and bloody disaster. Halfway through the seventeenth century the Jews found themselves in the middle of a national struggle between the Polish gentry and the Ukrainian cossacks, led by Hetman Chmielnicki. Hundreds of Jewish settlements and shtetlech were wiped out and their inhabitants massacred. At the same time the Jews in the west were caught in a war between the Poles and an invading army from Sweden. The result was again mass destruction of the population. But in spite of these difficulties, Jewish life managed to persevere, caught in the toils of endless persecution, economic restrictions, ritual accusations, expulsions, and forced conversions. What may have bolstered the Jews was the persistent and mystical belief that Poland was not an accidental station on their path to dispersion, but that it had been selected by fate. (There were legends that the Jews who were fleeing from Germany found a heavenly sent key that opened for them the territories of Eastern Europe.)

Poland was an independent state in union with Lithuania; in the latter part of the eighteenth century, it suffered a political collapse, and was divided by its three neighbors—Russia, Austria-Hungary, and Prussia. The shtetl entered into its final transformation at that time, and its socio-cultural pattern was stabilized for the next century and a half, till the end of its existence.

Russia, which seized the biggest slice of Poland, added hundreds of newly acquired Jewish settlements and townships to its Pale of Settlement, a narrow strip on its western border where the Jews were allowed to live. The other part of the Jewish population, incorporated into the Austro-Hungarian Empire, found itself in Galicia, Bohemia, Sub-Carpathia, Ruthenia, Bukovina, and Hungary. Jews in the former Polish province of Posen assimilated with the Prussian Jewish community.

The shtetl became exposed to the forces of different cultural influences. Like the biblical Jews who were divided into tribes according to their descent from the son of Jacob, the Eastern European Jews, still retaining the core of their traits, now underwent various regional transformations. They were called Litvaks or Galitzianer, Polishe, Ungarishe, Russishe, or Rumenishe Yiden according to whether they came from Lithuania, Galicia, Poland, Hungary, Russia or Rumania. These names persist till this day.

Everything in the shtetl—not only the people and their style of life but nature itself—was drawn into the orbit of Jewishness and endowed with Jewish characteristics. Animals, even plants, shared in the joys and anxieties of Jewish holidays. At the approach of the High Holydays, it was said, "fish trembled in the water" in the rivers of Poland. In the month of April blossoming trees and bushes were imagined to be "getting ready for Pesach." Trees standing still looked "like Jews during the prayer of the Eighteen Blessings." Trees moved by the wind were "swaying like Jews on the day of Yom Kippur." Striped animals were "wearing prayer shawls." Birds were not simply singing, they were singing *zmiroth* songs recited after a Sabbath meal. A rooster was crowing "like a hoarse *chazan* (cantor)." A goat's beard made him look like the rabbi; a sedentary cat was fat, lazy, and dumb like the wife of the shul's *gabbai* (synagogue trustee). To the writer Shalom Asch the "Weissel"—the river Vistula—"spoke Yiddish."

Since food fell into the province of special laws, it was unavoidable that in the shtetl many dishes would originate in conformance with certain dietary commandments. The influence of ingredients and recipes coming from neighboring cuisines also gave rise, in the shtetl, to such traditional dishes as gefillte fish, a minced fish dish with carrots, onions, and pepper; chopped herring, a splendid hors d'oeuvre of herring, apples, onions, and eggs; chopped, broiled chicken livers with chicken fat, eggs, and onions; *goldene yoich* (golden soup), chicken soup eaten by newlywed couples; *chremzlech,* a Passover dessert of matzoh flour pancakes filled with fruit; blintzes (better known among the Polish and Russian Jews as *mlinchkes*), pancakes filled with cheese or meat, folded and fried; *latkes,* pancakes made of grated potatoes at the time of the holiday Chanuka; *leykach,* honey cake for New Year, when people were supposed to eat something sweet; *lokshen,* a special type of noodle, usually made from eggs and flour; *miltz,* spleen stuffed with flour and raw onions; *tayglech,* a nut, honey, and ginger confection; *tsimmes,* a sweet side dish made usually from carrots and prunes or other dried fruit; and, of course, *chulent,* a traditional Sabbath meal prepared the day before (for cooking wasn't allowed on Sabbath) and made of beans, meat, potatoes, pearl barley, and sometimes prunes and seasoning.

To this day these dishes symbolize much more than food; they are symbols of Jewish identity, and very often the only thread of Jewish heritage for many contemporary Jews all over the world. Many of the foods were made especially for the certain holidays (like matzoh for Passover, *Homentaschen* for Purim, *Kreplach* filled with cheese for

Shevuot), but these prescriptions were not followed rigidly; most of the holiday dishes became part of the Jewish menu all year round.

The Jewish style of life affected Jewish clothing too. Religious commandments called for the *Taleth* (prayer shawl) and the *Taleth-Koten,* a fringed garment worn by all males, and yarmulkas. Women's fashion was particularly affected by religious traditions and customs. Women wore long skirts, long sleeves, high-buttoned collars. A married woman had to shave her head and wear a wig, the purpose being to make herself undesirable to other men; but the very art of making beautiful wigs defied this purpose, and the wig became an object of coquetry. Some of the men's clothing was influenced by non-Jewish neighbors, like the fur-trimmed hat (*shtraymel*) and the long kaftan, both of which were "borrowed" from the Polish gentry and the Ukrainians. Strict laws, imposed by the community, checked extravagance. Black was considered most appropriate for traditional garb. Incidentally, the first response of Jewish youth toward secularization was to dispense with traditional clothing and change into what was called a "European suit."

A special and interesting chapter in the story of the shtetl deals with the professions of its inhabitants. There were merchants, peddlers, and other middlemen. There was also a variety of craftsmen—cobblers, tailors, blacksmiths, glaziers, tanners, hat makers, wood hewers, carpenters, pitch dealers, teamsters, porters, milkmen, bakers, harness makers, and more. Tailors and cobblers were more likely to do repairs than to create new garments or shoes. Manual workers were generally looked upon with condescension, but some professions were held to be lower than others. For example, a water carrier was considered inferior to a carpenter, a tailor inferior to a watchmaker, for in each case the latter's work required brains. Actors and musicians were regarded with disdain, but here, too, subtle distinctions reigned. A violin was more respected than a drum, a cello more than a trumpet.

Apart from these general occupations and professions

were others—exclusively Jewish. Even here social connotations existed. Rabbis, ritual slaughterers, cantors, scribes, yeshivah teachers, and *mohels* (circumcisers) belonged to the *shayne yiden,* or the "beautiful Jews." Of lesser standing were the *shames* (beadle or sexton), the *cheder-melamed* (a teacher in a primary school), and the *belfer* (a man who helped bring the children to school). Still lower were the *Mikva-yid,* who served in the ritual bath, psalm sayers (who were hired to say psalms after a death), *El-Mole-Rachmim* makers (who "worked" in cemeteries saying, for a fee, prayers over a grave). Matchmakers (love was frowned upon as a non-Jewish invention), makers of *tsitsis* (fringed garments), *badchonim* (jesters who entertained at weddings), makers of *Havdole* candles (used with a special prayer at the end of Sabbath), feather pluckers (women who plucked freshly slaughtered kosher poultry; the feathers were used to stuff pillows and eiderdowns) were all uniquely Jewish occupations.

A shtetl could have professions still lower on the ladder of respectability. Robbers (who would seldom steal in their own shtetls, however), horse thieves, an occasional prostitute, living on the outskirts of the shtetl and serving a non-Jewish clientele, and border smugglers, if the shtetl was close to a border. Every child knew about these professionals and treated them appropriately.

Activity in the shtetl revolved around four or five main centers: the shul, the ritual bath, the home, the marketplace, and, in a sense, the cemetery.

In the synagogue the people prayed to God, studied the Talmud, and took part in functions related to the community. The public bath played a lesser but nonetheless important role; there the people met at least once a week in circumstances where they appeared before one another "as God created them," with none of the artificial distinctions that defined the social classes. These encounters no doubt influenced the shaping of the shtetl's human philosophy.

The home was the secluded cell where the Jew resided with his family, raising his children for the purpose of "marriage and good deeds," enjoying dignity and respect, and spending happy moments around the table celebrating the Sabbath, "the foretaste of the world to come," and other holidays. The home was not suspended in a vacuum. The whole community shared in the joys and sorrows, participated in the bar mitzvahs of the children, came to the weddings and the funerals. But the community was not just a passive witness; it judged the individual, often expressing approval or disapproval of his conduct. Indeed, the community exerted considerable control over the Jew's life. So strong was this self-imposed discipline that the shtetl had no need of a police force; if ever there were victims of thefts, swindles, or other crimes (murder was almost unheard of) complaints were seldom brought before non-Jewish authorities.

In the home the father was enveloped in respect. The aim of a family was to have "*naches* (joy) from its children." It was the dream of each parent to have a son become a scholar and a daughter the wife of a scholar. Parents raised and readily helped their children even after they were married; but it was considered a tragedy to be helped by them. And, speaking of children, the shtetl was the birthplace of the Jewish mother. She hovered over her children, overfeeding them, overcautioning them about their health and safety, pushing them to study. All this was quite justified in the hazardous world of the shtetl, where food was scarce, health was precarious, safety was in constant peril, and studying was the "crown of life." When these motherly characteristics were carried over into the different conditions of new countries, the "Jewish mother" became irritating and a pest.

The cemetery, in the language of the shtetl, "the House of Life," was a place for the dead, but it also played an important role for the living. The dead were not just memories. It was believed that deceased relatives and friends were always waiting in their graves, ready to be of assistance. They were in a privileged position to help, for they were closer to the source of divine justice. In time of distress, sickness, epidemics, pogroms, and even bankruptcy, it was customary to run to the cemetery, cry at the graves of the more pious and, therefore, more influential dead, and ask their

14

help. Dead relatives were also invited to weddings and other joyful events.

Of course, the marketplace was exceedingly important in the life of the shtetl. Here was the source of its livelihood. Here the Jews, who always lived amongst themselves, came in contact with their non-Jewish neighbors. Here the peasants of the neighboring villages came to sell their products, buy urban products from the Jews, and use the services of the Jewish artisans. In the course of centuries this contact was seldom of lasting duration or of profound value. The relationship usually remained on the level of mutual distrust. To the Jew, the non-Jew was the symbol of raw instinct, of physical power and primitive reflexes. To the peasant, the Jew represented slyness, brains, and, most of all, religious heresy. The peasant's life was dominated by churches and chapels, by figures erected on the crossroads symbolizing God, the Mother of God, and the saints—all of them in concrete human shapes. In this respect the Jews were a complete mystery since the peasant could see no evidence of a Jewish God. He may have ventured to cast a glance through the window of a shul where he saw no statues of divinity. Instead of holy pictures, the Jew had mysterious mezuzahs on the door post of his home. The peasant saw a Jew praying, wrapped in an exotic shawl, wearing a little black box on his forehead and arm; he heard strange words muttered in a dark language. This unknown created the usual fear and hatred.

There were instances when a non-Jew would be invited to a Jewish home for a festival or a wedding. It also happened that a wandering Jewish peddler, looking for bargains in the villages, would stay overnight in a non-Jewish farm. But these instances did not mean very much. The marketplace, the stage for contacts, could also become the breeding spot for bloody riots.

Much has been written about Jewish humor. The mistake most often committed is to see it as "a thing in itself," instead of viewing it in perspective against the background of the shtetl. The Jew, faced with the non-Jewish hostile world, had to acknowledge its physical superiority—how could he deny it?—but he could denigrate it intellectually. He had no way of answering violence with violence, so he chose as his weapon the "fist of humor." A pathetic weapon? But the only one available: "One day a peasant asked his Jewish neighbor: why is it that Jews are so clever? "Because we eat a special sort of herring," replied the Jew. "Would I become clever if I ate a piece of that herring?" "Sure, but it's very expensive. It costs a hundred rubles a piece." A hundred rubles was a fortune, but the peasant paid the price. As soon as he took the first bite, he exclaimed, "but it's just an ordinary herring. I can get it for a kopeck." "You see," replied the Jew, "you hardly tasted it and you are already wiser than before."

There are thousands of these little stories in which the weak but clever Jew outsmarts the strong goy. Some believe the source of all these jokes was the biblical Book of Esther, in which the wise Mordechai saved his fellow Jews in ancient Persia from extermination planned by the powerful but brainless Haman. If this was the grandfather of Jewish humor, then all the rest of the Jewish jokes are its descendants; in the precarious condition of the Jews in the marketplace and their dangerous physical contact with the goy, it was comforting to them to keep in mind the story of the wise Mordechai and the shameful end of the wicked Haman.

The fact that the shtetl came to an end in the gas chambers of Auschwitz and Treblinka has tinted much of the attitude of those who write on this subject. Even those who have endeavored the almost impossible task of remaining neutral have not avoided a certain subjectivity. Others have consciously seen the life of the shtetl in terms of holiness.

The shtetl, they claim, was attached to eternity, to God, and unaffected by the outside world. The shtetl was not a place where the Jews chose to live, but a temporary stage on which they were placed to perform His divine will. The struggle for physical existence had one purpose only: to preserve the life of the spirit. The main function was to serve God; the only hope was the coming of the Messiah. The commercial dealings, the manual work, the fight for daily bread, were no more than the frame which held together the content; and the content was the spirit. The laws of the country, even the privileges given by the rulers, were only means to sustain existence. Life was lived, not by the rules from outside, but by inner discipline, and this discipline made the individual responsible to the sole judge, God. The relation with God was overwhelming and intimate. It had begun with the Covenant of Abraham, and it continued, in its pure and unadulterated form, for the succeeding generations.

The Jew's relation with God consisted of direct dealings, prayers, rituals, or fasting and permeated every aspect of daily life, from the moment of getting up in the morning until bedtime, from the moment of birth till the moment of death. It also "acted" in the hours of sleep and extended over the grave. The week has seven days; six of them were given to prepare for the seventh, the day of Sabbath. The seventh day was considered a sample of the life to come.

The birth of a male child was a reason for joy, for it was the fulfillment of the promise of the continuation of the Jewish people. On the eighth day the child was circumcised, a mark of the covenant between Abraham and God. At the age of three he was carried, wrapped in a prayer shawl, to the *cheder,* where he began the long journey of education. At thirteen he became bar mitzvah, which meant that from then on all his good deeds and sins would no longer be charged to the account of his father. The birth of a girl also was a reason for joy, though to a lesser extent. She didn't count as much as a boy (in his daily prayers each Jew thanked the Creator for not having made him a woman), but as she would become the wife of a Jew, she would, indirectly, have a part in the purpose of this world. Each step in life was taken in harmony with a general pattern. When a man died he "gathered into his ancestors."

The shtetl was a place of sacredness. Each shtetl actually called itself *kehilla kedosha*—a holy community. (In official documents of the community organizations the name of each shtetl was preceded by the two letters k.k.—*kehilla kedosha*. And so it was never simply Radom, Rowno, or Tarnow, but k.k. Radom, k.k. Rowno, etc.) "The world," says the distinguished Jewish theologian and philosopher Abraham Joshua Heschel, "was important because houses of study existed in it . . . Their life was oriented to the spiritual and they could therefore ignore its external aspects . . . The little Jewish communities in Eastern Europe were like sacred texts opened before the eyes of God . . . Study was a technique for sublimating feelings into thought, for transposing dreams into syllogisms, for expressing grief in difficult theoretical formulations, and joy—by finding a solution to a difficult passage in Maimonides."

The most valuable thing in even the poorest Jewish home was the bookshelf, filled with holy books. In the home of a learned man there would be an armoire filled with volumes bound in leather and stamped with gilded letters; in the house of a pauper there would at least be a prayer book and, probably, a book of psalms. While the great majority of the outside world's citizens—kings, their gentry, even some of the clergy—could neither read nor write, every Jewish child at the age of three began learning the alphabet.

Even the most ardent of these "sanctifiers" of the shtetl would not deny that life there was poor, destitute, bordering on misery. But this, they say, was only the outer shell. Inside each shtetl was a kingdom of the spirit. They may also admit that the subject of study often was irrelevant to one's life, that offering sacrifices in the biblical Temple or studying ancient agricultural laws had no relationship to the present. But this was not the point. Study was never done for practical purposes. It "provided the double joy: the joy of recreation and the opportunity to escape from the world."

Such is the attitude of those who see the shtetl in terms

of holiness. But how true is it? Indeed, how impervious was Jewish life to the environment, and how long did this imperviousness last? How true is it that all the Jews in Eastern Europe were concerned, not with how to exist, but with the essence and purpose of existence?

The question is not whether the shtetl was a holy text or not, but rather whether the inhabitants themselves accepted it as such. Did they consider themselves happy with their role of being a part of this life of holiness without regard to the position they were assigned? Were the poor, the *proste yiden* or "simple Jews," as content with their poverty as the rich were with their wealth? Was everybody content, not only with the place in society assigned to him by God, but with God himself?

Those who differ strongly with the view of the "sanctifiers" admit that many of the fine qualities attributed to the shtetl did exist, but that these qualities should be viewed with less romanticism. Scholarship was one of the foundations of the shtetl's life, but was not scholasticism a better term? It is true that the shtetl was surrounded by an ocean of illiteracy, with the peasants and gentry unable to read or write while each Jewish child was launched on the road of education, starting with the Hebrew alphabet and moving to the complexities of law and ancient philosophy; but to be fair, stress has to be placed on the word "ancient" rather than on the word "philosophy." Critics point to the shtetl's total detachment from actual life. A spiritual kingdom? Perhaps. But a bizarre monarchy, suspended in a void.

As for the inner structure of the shtetl, it was hardly a picture of harmony. It was socially divided: the wealthy versus the poor, the learned versus the humble, those who were "soaked" in *yichus,* or "prestige," versus the pariahs. True, the gap between the social groups inside was relatively narrower than the gap which separated them from the outside world. The man who was rich, a man of leisure in the shtetl, might be considered a pauper if judged by the standards of the world outside. But the shtetl was perhaps the only place in the world where a division existed between "beautiful" and "simple"—*shayne yiden* and *proste yiden.* "Beautiful" was by no means an esthetic quality. A "beautiful Jew" might be lame, one-eyed, and hunchbacked but maintain a high position in the community, his prominence due either to material possession or to learning, or both. The *proste yiden* were the opposite—the poor, the uneducated, the manual laborers, and the beggars.

Strangely enough, despite the "kingdom of spirit," or perhaps because of it, this social stratification was most visible in the one place where everybody was supposed to be equal before God: the shul. Here the seating of the congregation was arranged in a way that clearly reflected the social position of every worshiper. The honored eastern wall, against which the Holy Ark stood, was reserved for the most prominent and respected. The *shayne yiden* occupied the seats close to the Holy Scrolls. Behind them sat the ordinary Jewish *balebatim* (householders), and far, far behind were the *proste.*

Learning was held in high esteem. The dream of a wealthy merchant was to marry his daughter to an outstanding scholar, a destitute but brilliant yeshivah student. But, as a consequence, this respect for spiritual values created disdain for those—tailors, shoemakers, blacksmiths —who earned their living with their hands. Sometimes there were separate shuls for artisans and craftsmen in order not to mix the *shayne* with the *proste.*

To suppose that the *proste yiden* stoically accepted their lot would deprive them of an elementary degree of social patience, human dignity, and their proverbial sense of humor. There were no uprisings, no barricades, no Bastille-like stormings of the eastern wall in the shul, such violence having no place in the shtetl's pattern. But the spirit of rebellion was there, and it found its outlets in the shtetl's folklore, humor, proverbs, sayings, and folk songs.

To live in misery, to be threatened with constant peril, and at the same time to be told that they were the Chosen People was grotesque for the Jews of the shtetl. Even the most serious man was tempted to see "chosen" as a ques-

20

tionable compliment, bordering on the absurd. He could easily discover a whole series of similar incongruities. If "chosen" could be accompanied by misery, then perhaps learning could go with vanity, piety with bigotry, wealth with lesser virtues.

Normally, questions like these could trigger a wave of skepticism, disbelief, and open opposition; but in the conditions of the shtetl skepticism was funneled into more peaceful though thorny channels: witticisms and satire. It is enough to skim the surface of Jewish folklore to discover a wealth of such material. One of the classic anecdotes born in the shtetl contains enough spice to comprise a whole Communist Manifesto.

It is a variation on a biblical story and has three parts. Part one is a summary of the episode: after spending forty days and nights on the mountain of Sinai, Moses came down to present the Children of Israel with the two tablets containing the Ten Commandments. But here, to his shock, he saw the Israelites dancing around a Golden Calf. In dismay Moses threw the tablets to the ground, breaking them into fragments.

Part two tells us that the Tablets broke in such a way that some fragments contained the words "thou shalt not" while others contained the words "kill," "steal," or "commit adultery." Seeing these fragments, the Children of Israel began gathering them up; and it happened some got hold of the words "thou shalt not" while the others picked up "steal" and "kill." Those who got "thou shalt not" became the future *proste yiden,* and those with "steal" and "kill" became the *shayne yiden.*

Part three says, when the Messiah comes the broken fragments will reunite and it will again be "thou shalt not steal," "thou shalt not kill."

The anecdote, explaining the origin of the privileged and the paupers in the shtetl, may not be as brief as the usual Jewish joke, but it is loaded with social dynamite. Part three may mellow the spice of part two, crowning it with the ultimate vision of the Messiah, but it doesn't erase the account of the origin of the *shayne yiden.*

These signs of dissatisfaction contradict the belief, held by some writers of Jewish history, that "with all the chaos around, inside was a system of order." The shakiness of the order found its expression not only in folklore, but in a much wider and more serious outlet—the great religious and later secular dissents.

Shtetl humor abounds in hundreds of such stories, which always have two protagonists, a rich man and a beggar, a pious man and a simple believer, a learned man and an unlearned one. The wealthy man is always presented as a glutton or miser whereas the poor is warm and wise; the pious is a bigot and the simple believer is honest and straight; the learned is devious and a hypocrite while the unlearned is pure and virtuous. None of these anecdotes calls for a revolution. They have a tepid temperature of good-natured derision, but even the mockery, mild as it is, points to a sharp social awareness.

The shtetl immortalized living symbols of social rebels. Its folklore lists a number of pranksters who, like Robin Hood or Till Eulenspigel, ridiculed the rich and the mighty. There are enough delightful tales about them to fill volumes. The same spirit of discontent gave birth to another form of social indignation, hundreds of sharp and thorny sayings, many directed against the rich. "The rich man's foolishness is more admired than the poor man's wisdom." "A foolish rich man is still a lord." "The rich man has his brain in the wallet." Or, in the same vein, a rather weak consolation, "Shrouds have no pockets." Spears against bigots are sharper. "The tavern cannot corrupt the good man, the synagogue cannot reform the bad one." "The rabbi drains the bottle and tells others to be dry." "Better good than pious." "Don't fast and don't steal." "Better a Jew without a beard than a beard without a Jew." "The nearer the shul, the further from God."

It was almost unavoidable that God himself would come in for some cautious evaluation. After all, the Jews suffered on His behalf; surely they were entitled to some intimacy, to get a little angry, even sarcastic. "If God were living on earth people would break his windows." "God is a giver; if He doesn't give a sickness, He will certainly give a disease." "God is an honest repayer—but He is in no hurry." "God loves the poor but helps the rich." Then a direct statement: "You created a world—such a year on me; You rule it—such a year on my enemies."

Though for centuries God had remained in the hands of scholars who kept Him in an area of abstract study, making Him unapproachable, the middle of the eighteenth century saw the emergence of a religious movement that demanded a renewal of the intimacy with God. The shtetl's inhabitants wanted a new way of belief and a rebirth of enthusiasm. The stagnant way of learning became an obstacle. There was an accumulated passion for God and a suppressed ecstasy that was in need of relief. The new movement was called Hasidism, and its founder was a man who was called the Baal Shem Tov. He preached the simple but forgotten truth that everybody was equal before God, the learned as well as the unlearned. He taught that a pure heart was superior to study, that the act of prayer was not necessarily the repetition of stagnant phrases or lines from books. It could be done by singing and dancing. Still more, one could pray not only with one's soul, but with one's body. The Psalmist's exclamation, "I pray to you with all my bones," meant an end to the division of body and soul; man regained his entity, the gulf between sacred and profane was bridged. Now the humble could achieve a total integration with the divine. Thus the movement of Hasidism came to be a democratic revolution in which "the poor of the earth" were elevated to the level of partners with God.

Hasidism carried the seeds of its own destruction, however, by creating leaders who called themselves *Zadikim* (righteous ones). A number of dynasties of these leaders emerged, and they fought among themselves for influence and power; rabbis established themselves as miracle workers and mediators between man and God. This resulted in another oligarchy, which in turn was attacked by new opponents.

Then another powerful movement appeared, the Haskala, which mocked Hasidism, accusing it of spreading superstitions and paganism. Haskala, which originated in the west, attempted to turn the face of the shtetl toward the "world," to infuse into Jewish life modern philosophy and modern thought, to relieve education from the "chains" of theology and begin the teaching of secular subjects, to do away with escapism, to accept life as it was. The followers of Haskala wanted to change Jewish life. The slogan of the Haskala was: "Be a Jew at home and a man in the street." It was a movement of reform, not of assimilation.

Haskala brought forth modern Yiddish literature and the elevation of Yiddish as a language. Up till then Yiddish had been considered jargon, the language of women, and a helpful means of communicating in day-to-day dealings. Serious writing was done in Hebrew, which was called *loshen kodesh*, "a holy language." Those who wished to reeducate the masses were compelled to use their language, Yiddish. So an extraordinary thing occurred: the first writers who used Yiddish as a didactic tool fell under its spell and transformed its use into a wonderful art. The man who is called the grandfather of modern Yiddish literature, Mendele Moycher Seforim (Shalom Yakov Abramovitch), went through several stages. He set out to use the despised jargon for the purpose of satirizing the stagnancy of Jewish life, but he soon found himself "trapped" in the wonders of the language. On his way to becoming a sarcastic, condescending preacher, he became an artist.

Finally, for the first time in the life of the shtetl, there emerged two big political movements: Zionism and Socialism. Both came almost at the same time, and though opposed to each other, they were consistent with the shtetl's basic beliefs.

Zionism was a movement of temperament rather than of political logic. It was a state of impatience. It tried to transform the traditional saying, "Next year in Jerusalem," which every Jew repeated in his daily prayers, from its Messianic connotation into a political slogan. Today it would read "Jerusalem NOW!" Zionism professed to do away with the age-old attraction to the Polish soil, regarding the Jews' long period of suffering in Eastern Europe as a vain struggle of aliens on an alien soil. The shtetl was an escape from reality, so Zionism proclaimed the escape from the shtetl—geographically only, without destroying the contents of the shtetl's life. The ideal of Zionism was to create a Jewish state in which one could retain the Jewish virtues without accepting the world's vices. Considering Yiddish as a product of exile, Zionism rejected it, choosing Hebrew instead as the tongue of the future state. This would give the feeling of direct continuation with the days of the Bible, and the land of the Bible. Thus, Zionism was the fulfillment of the old divine promise of the Ingathering of the People.

In the beginning the movement seemed more a dream than an attainable reality; it therefore attracted only a few of the educated. The Jewish masses were less patient. "Messiah NOW" was not sufficient; the call should sound out "Messiah NOW and RIGHT HERE." Another political movement therefore appeared, the Jewish socialist movement which called itself Bund.

Bund spread among the poor, among those to whom deliverance was an urgent need. Its teachings were attractive, for they sounded practical: deliverance was not a matter for the future, but for the present. The Messiah was not waiting for the divine sign to start riding toward Jerusalem on his white donkey. He lived in the hearts of all men, and they could bring their deliverance upon themselves.

While studying the teachings of Marx and Engels, Lassale and Medem, the Jewish poor in the shtetl saw how smoothly the new teachings fitted into the words of the ancient prophets. "You have nothing to lose but your chains." "Workers of all countries, unite." "No more wars." Wasn't it exactly what the prophet meant when he talked about lions lying down with lambs, and of beating swords into plowshares? Many of the young Bundists from the crowded, poor streets of the shtetl, educated on the Talmud, didn't actually have such a long way to go. Later, when the Bund became a powerful party with its own candidates for the Polish parliament and municipal bodies, thousands of religious Jews gave their votes to those "godless socialists." They were not frightened of the sharp slogans, for they sounded familiar. They had heard them from the prophets.

More important, Jewish socialism did not reject Yiddish. There was no need to make an acrobatic jump of two thousand years to attach oneself to biblical ancestors, to renounce one's tongue. The emerging Yiddish literature demonstrated that this language was no jargon; it took its place beside the other languages of the world.

At the end of the nineteenth century the shtetl opened up to ideas that generated from its inner life and were influenced by mysticism, Hasidism, Haskala, Zionism, and Bundism. The old shtetl began to change radically under the impact of often contradictory forces.

It was at this time that two million Jews from Eastern Europe, driven by pogroms and political and economic oppressions, began a large-scale emigration to the West, mostly to the United States. Sometimes shtetls, with their total populations, boarded grim cattle ships in order to reach the "gold-paved" streets of New York. Here they first went through the hell of Castle Garden to discover that the promised gold was sweat and tears; but the consolation was freedom. In the new country they realized that the shtetl had accompanied them. Neighbors who had come before them had created a substitute for the shtetl, which they called *landsmanshaft.* Members called themselves brethren. If a man came from the shtetl Radzymin, he would found a society of Radzyminer; if he came from a still smaller and obscure place like Frampol, he instantly became a Frampoler. A *landsmanshaft* was not the same as a shtetl, but from now on he knew that he would be surrounded by his old neighbors who would come to his children's bar mitzvahs, would visit in the hospital, would help him, if necessary, with a loan; and after a hundred and twenty years, he would come to rest, not just among Jews, but among his townsmen.

Meanwhile, in Eastern Europe the First World War

ended with the Bolshevik Revolution and the rebirth of an independent Poland. The Revolution brought an end to the Pale of Settlement; from then on Jews could live where they pleased. But the Revolution also brought an end to the socio-cultural structure of the shtetl. The new order realized some of the shtetl's old hopes, but it augmented its fears, too. The new rulers forced upon it a new life, destroying its structure, uprooting its ideas, trampling upon its old values. For the Jews caught in the new regime the order was a "culture—national in form and socialist in content." Years later came the annihilation of Jewish life—form and content—by the murderous terror of Stalin, under the guise of the promises of the Revolution.

Between the two world wars Jewish life went through a period of amazing renaissance in independent Poland, a period never experienced before except perhaps in Spain. Never before was the cultural life so rich. Yiddish literature flourished; for the first time Jewish political parties became a power in the political constellation of the country. Jewish life seemed to dig deeper roots than ever before. The Jewish masses achieved highest standards of education. While the parents and grandparents were still flocking to the "courts" of their Hasidic rabbis—to Kotzk, Ger, Kozhenitz, or Skernevitz—their children discovered a new kind of Zadikim. The books were no longer *Sefer Chasidim* (the *Book of the Righteous*) of Rabeynu Yehuda Hachasid, the *Shevet Musar (Rod of Reproof)* of Reb Eliyohu ben Abraham Hakohen, or *Likutei Mohoran (Excerpts of Reb Nachman)* by Reb Nachman Bratzlaver. The new books were *Das Kapital* of Marx, *Fields, Factories and Workshops* by Piotr Alekseyevich Kropotkin, *Altneuland* by Theodor Herzl, and even *What is to be Done?* by Lenin.

As a rule, only the leaders and a few intellectuals could get into the profound depths of these books. The young men and women had the same awe for these formidable-sounding books as their fathers had had for theirs. For the first time the marketplace in the shtetl was not the sole meeting place between Jews and non-Jews. The streets in the larger cities saw tens of thousands of Jewish workers marching in solidarity with Polish workers, displaying the same red flags—isn't blood of the same color?—and singing songs different in language but of identical content: "Brethren and sisters of misery and toil."

Over the border, in the west, a man with a ridiculous mustache was preparing the shtetl's Final Solution.

Those who denigrate the shtetl as archaic commit the error of applying the standards of today to the times of yesteryear, standards of industrial and material societies to a society which ignored material values, cherishing those of the spirit. For how can we even try to share the beliefs of those to whom belief was the foundation of existence?

It often seems that the life style of the shtetl was of such uniqueness that it was made up of hieroglyphics accessible only to those initiated in the art of decoding. But this is hardly true. The most Jewish of all the Jewish writers, Sholom Aleichem, was completely engulfed in the shtetl's life. All his characters are drawn from the shtetl, its traditions, customs, conventions, idioms, gestures, and superstitions. Accordingly, he should remain inaccessible to anybody who has not been totally familiar with this jungle of symbols. Yet the works of Sholom Aleichem have been translated into languages not only geographically close to the shtetl, Russian, Polish, French, German, and English, but also translated, read, and loved by readers as far away as China. *Fiddler on the Roof,* drawn from his central work *Tevye the Dairyman,* was played before Catholic nuns in New York, Hindus in London, and Japanese in Tokyo. Black kids from a high school in Brooklyn played with wonderful affinity the characters of Tevye, Golda, and Chava; their parents laughed and cried along with the inhabitants of the Yiddish shtetl of Anatevka who became dear to the hearts of audiences around the world.

"Heart" is a word which we have learned to regard with suspicion, but this, too, was one of the underlying qualities of the shtetl. A great compliment one could pay in a shtetl was to say that a man had "a Jewish head." But a still greater compliment was that he had "a Jewish heart." This was the prevailing sentiment in that extinguished world: kindness, sympathy to the poor, to the children, the weak, and the insulted. Despite their social differences, the inhabitants of the shtetl were all "little people," *kleine menschelech.* This was the title of the first novel of Mendele Moycher Seforim, and it is no accident that this novel has been accepted as the foundation of modern Yiddish literature. It also explains, perhaps, why these "little people" have such an appeal to the people of the wide world.

On all its torturous stages, life in the shtetl went through a cavalcade of changes: from a total obedience to God, to mysticism and Hasidism, to Haskala or Zionism or Socialism or Communism or Anarchism. These changes were not genetic mutations but part of an evolution. The same Covenant of Abraham made in times of legend ran repeatedly through all the transformations into the future. The old forms were crumbling, but those who had "an eye to see and heart to feel" knew that the new forms would always emerge with the core intact.

It can be said that up to the last moment of its terrible death, the shtetl preserved the innocence it possessed at its beginning. The Jews who had arrived seven or eight hundred years earlier believed that the earth where they came to settle down was chosen for them by their God. "Polen" to settle down was chosen for them by their God. Poland, in Yiddish "Polen," was composed of the two Hebrew words: *po* and *lin*—"here shall we spend the night." Nobody could have forseen that this phrase which expressed so much hope could materialize in such an appalling way.

That it would mean "Night" in its most horrible sense.

THE SHTETL

A shtetl was a small town in Eastern Europe which contained all the elements of a community: streets, houses, public buildings, places for trade, for study, and for worship. But while each shtetl was a little town, the opposite cannot be said: that each little town was a shtetl. For a shtetl, from its conception hundreds of years ago until its tragic end in this century, was more than the sum of its physical ingredients; it also possessed an additional, intangible quality which transformed a township into a shtetl—for its Jewish inhabitants at least.

There are various theories as to what this quality was: religion, philosophy, style of life, sum of beliefs, or historical fate. But whatever it was, it was able to tie its inhabitants to their legendary past, subject them to an inner discipline and turn their hopes toward a mystical future.

Opposite: Children fetching water.

During a break between services men gather in the sunshine outside a shul.

Above: A village band.
Opposite: Jewish volunteer firemen in a Lithuanian town.

36

Above: All the men of a Polish town turned out to give a farewell party to their preacher who is leaving for America. Opposite: Distinguished elders of the community of Chelm. In folklore Chelm was the butt of many jokes as a city inhabited solely by fools.

Typical old houses in Poland. Top: in the town of Opatow. Bottom: in Lublin.
Opposite: A young bagel peddler in Warsaw.

38

Right: The most prominent citizens of a shtetl assemble for a group portrait. Far right: A poor man eating with a wooden spoon out of an iron pot. Below: Inmates of a home for the aged in Vilna studying the Talmud.

On Purim a band of Jewish musicians in Knyszyn, Poland, dressed in military uniforms and performed to raise money for charity.

43

Left: A group of Galician Jews in a park.
Below: The famous "Tlomackie" synagogue in Warsaw.

Above: In a Rumanian town a social gathering around a festive table. Opposite top: The wooden Bialystok house in which the inventor of the international language Esperanto, Dr. Ludwig Zamenhof, was born. Opposite bottom: A typical street in Pinsk.

48

Left: In the winter cold a water carrier gets his day's water supply from a village well. Opposite: The *Shabbath-Klapper* had the special job of knocking on house shutters throughout the shtetl to announce the arrival of the Sabbath.

Opposite: Two attendants beside a boiler used for heating the water at a ritual bath.
Below: Selling geese in a Warsaw market; the geese were kept in boxes or baskets.

Left: A *cheder* teacher with his pupils.
Below: On his way to school a boy buys an apple from a street peddler.

Above: An apartment interior; this kitchen served five families. Opposite: A housewife in her kitchen; at her right is a saltbox containing the salt used in making meat kosher.

Clockwise, from left:
A woman beside her daughter's gravestone; in the village street a peddler of kindling wood drinking a cup of tea brought to him by his wife; a porter; a butcher leading a calf to slaughter.

An old man taking the sun in a courtyard. Center: One of the first Yiddish theaters in Poland, the "Muranower Teyater" in Warsaw. Opposite: Booksellers in the court of the old shul in Vilna.

Clockwise, from above: Nalewki Gass, the main street in the Jewish quarter of Warsaw; the marketplace in Slonim; a corner of the Jewish section of Luck, Volhynia, with a church looming over it; children in a Lublin street.

62

Opposite top: The town droshky driver of Ciechanow, Poland. Opposite bottom: A winter scene in the slums inhabited by Jewish poor in Grodno. Above: A dinner for the shtetl poor paid for as an act of charity by a woman who recovered from an illness.

Above: The Society for Providing Dowries for Poor Brides in Sandomierz, Poland.
Opposite top: A wedding, with the wedding canopy set up under the open skies.
Opposite bottom: Jewish musicians playing at a Polish wedding.

Right: Poland's only beardless rabbi—a man who was forced to shave because of a skin disease. Opposite top: The old cemetery in Vilna where the famous scholar the Vilna Gaon is interred. Opposite bottom: School children playing around a well. Below: The main street in Lukow, Poland.

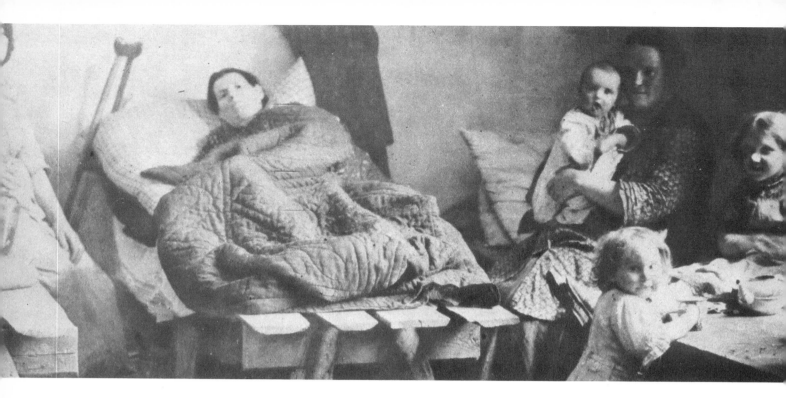

Left: The Jewish woman lying in bed was crippled when Russian soldiers threw her from a moving train. Opposite bottom: The main street in Nowy Dwor, Poland, during a flood. Below: A poor family after being evicted from their home in Bialystok.

70

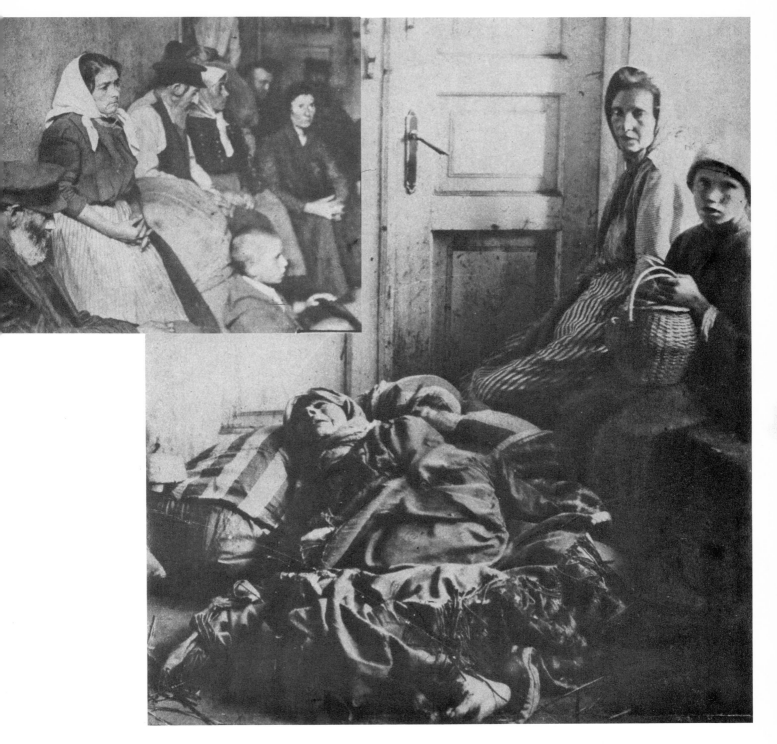

Opposite and above: Jews from the Lithuanian city of Kovno exiled during World War I by the Russian army.

CHILDREN

It is often said about children of the shtetl that they were "miniature Jews"—young in age and small in size, but carrying all the burdens and worries of adults. This, if not altogether true, was so to a great extent. The span of childhood in a shtetl was indeed short. Boys at the age of three were carried, wrapped in their father's prayer shawls, to the cheder to begin their long years of study; girls at a very early age were already hard-working helpers in their homes.

Despite all this, children in the shtetl, like children all over the world, even when yoked to responsibilities and chores, knew how to turn the burdens into play.

Opposite: Boys getting water from the town pump.

74

Left: Two yeshivah boys studying. Below: A blind beggar is led through the streets by his son, singing for a coin or a piece of bread.

Above: Jewish girls were free from the obligation of studying the Torah but were still expected to pray. Here two girls are being taught to read from a prayer book. Opposite: A schoolroom scene; there is one book for five students.

78

Left: Young boys selling pottery at the marketplace in Opatow. Right: Two orphaned sisters who lived in a basement. Below: A sister and brother from a more prosperous family. Opposite bottom: Two yeshivah boys.

80

Opposite: A young boy wearing his handkerchief around his neck because no one is allowed to carry handkerchiefs in a pocket on the Sabbath. Below: Schoolboys playing with an abandoned horse cart.

Opposite: Two schoolboys share one piece of bread. Below:
A kindergarten in a Carpathian village; one of the youngsters
is obviously wearing his father's fringed garment, or *tsitsis*.

Work and play. Above: Youngsters unloading a coal wagon. Left: A twelve-year-old cabman in Otwotzk, a summer resort frequented by Warsaw Jews. Right: Five schoolboys posed on the rungs of a ladder.

85

In this *cheder* in Lublin, Poland, the "students" can hardly reach the table.

88   Above: A brother and sister getting a supply of water for their family in Krakow, Poland. Opposite top: A rabbi and his aides on a visit to an orphanage in Radom, Poland. Opposite bottom: A troop of young warriors in Opatow, Poland, armed with sticks and ready for battle.

In Dej, Rumania, both the faculty and the students turned out for this school picture. The children's manner of dress was characteristic of this part of Eastern Europe.

WOMEN

In the shtetl Jewish women did not fully share spiritual responsibilities and privileges along with the men. Women were free of the obligation to study and to perform many religious acts, but this being "free" was not an expression of freedom; it provided, instead, a proof of their lesser social stature. Even in the after life, it was believed, men were to sit among the Glorious Righteous on comfortable armchairs, while their wives were to serve as their footstools. From an egalitarian standpoint, Jewish women were a pitiable and underprivileged group. But viewed within the context of the shtetl's total life, the woman's role was not at all inferior to the man's.

While it is true that only the man was engaged in direct contact with God, his contact could hardly be attained without the women's support and care. To the general pattern of the shtetl's life the woman contributed her share of softness, steadfastness, subtlety, and human warmth—as well as the symbol of her virtue.

Opposite: A young girl watching her mother at work in the kitchen.

Women at work. Above: At the vegetable market. Opposite: Washing clothes in a creek. Opposite bottom: An eighty-five-year-old mother and her daughter spinning thread.

94

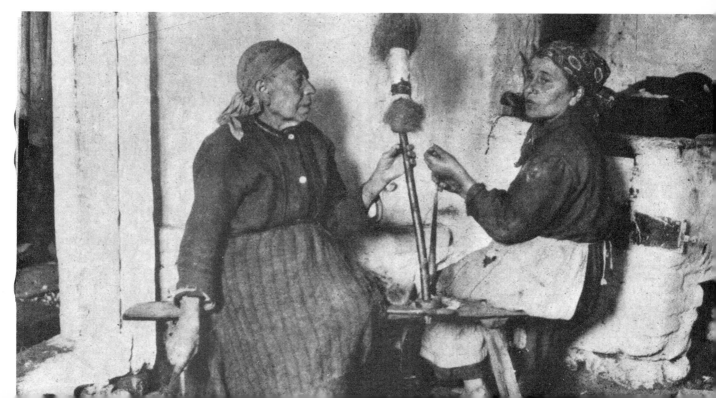

Below: Two elderly women shopping for Sabbath. Opposite: An old woman opening the door of her stove. This sort of stove was used mainly for heating; the niche at the top could be used for keeping food warm.

Above: A woman and her daughters, who made their living
by baking and selling bread. Opposite: An elderly woman and
her grandchild, whose father has emigrated to America.

Above: A woman deserted by her husband, who left her with five children. Opposite top: A quartet of Warsaw women; three of them wear the frilly caps often worn by pious old women. Right: A Jewish farm woman in Czechoslovakia separating flax fibre from the straw—one of the first steps in the tedious process of making linen.

100

Opposite: A housewife dishing out dinner. Below: Three sisters of Odessa dressed in the latest fashions at the turn of the century. Right: A fashionable and prosperous young belle from Dvinsk, Latvia.

103

HASIDIM

The Hasidic movement is usually seen in terms of philosophy and religion. Actually, it originated as a social movement, directed against an oligarchy of scholars who had monopolized the Jewish God, making Him inaccessible to the simple and unlearned. The founders of Hasidism liberated the ordinary man's suppressed longing for God, and brought Him down from the remote reaches of heaven, to a place where unlearned men could approach Him. Now, the road to God was no longer obstructed by barricades of unfathomable writings; it stood open to anyone who possessed faith, who could express it in the simplest prayers and even in unverbalized states of elation and joy.

By preaching all men's equality before God, Hasidism was a profoundly democratic movement that exerted a great influence on many aspects of shtetl life.

Opposite: At a summer resort, the Rebbe of Kozienice, Poland, takes a walk with two of his beadles.

105

Below: Three elderly Hasidim on a Sabbath day in Warsaw.
Opposite: Hasidim enjoy a stroll on the grounds of the Gerer Rebbe's villa.

107

108

Opposite top: The beadle of the old shul in Radom, Poland, and his wife, dressed in their holiday clothes. Opposite bottom: A group of Galician Hasidim in Przemysl, Poland. Below: A few "secular" hats can be seen on the hundreds of Hasidim who have come to celebrate the wedding of the Gerer Rebbe's son.

Clockwise, from above: The rabbi of Stolin on the way to his son's wedding; on his right is an attendant, a Hasid in Cossack dress, riding a horse; a sixty-year-old Hasid in his characteristic Galician hat; a seventy-year-old follower of the Kotzker Rebbe; the Rebbe of Ger with two sextons out for an airing in the resort of Marienbad.

Opposite: Hasidim
sitting on a bench
looking on proudly at
a little boy, who is
the son of their
Rebbe. Above: The
head of a yeshivah
conducting a class.
Right: A white-
bearded Hasidic rabbi
and three of his fol-
lowers out for a walk,
carrying umbrellas
in case of rain.

The famous Rebbe of Belz (wearing a fur hat) surrounded by some of his followers in the resort of Marienbad.

Above: Returning from shul on a frosty Sabbath. Opposite: Yeshivah boys are learning the textile trade in a school of the ORT, a Jewish organization which preaches the dignity of work.

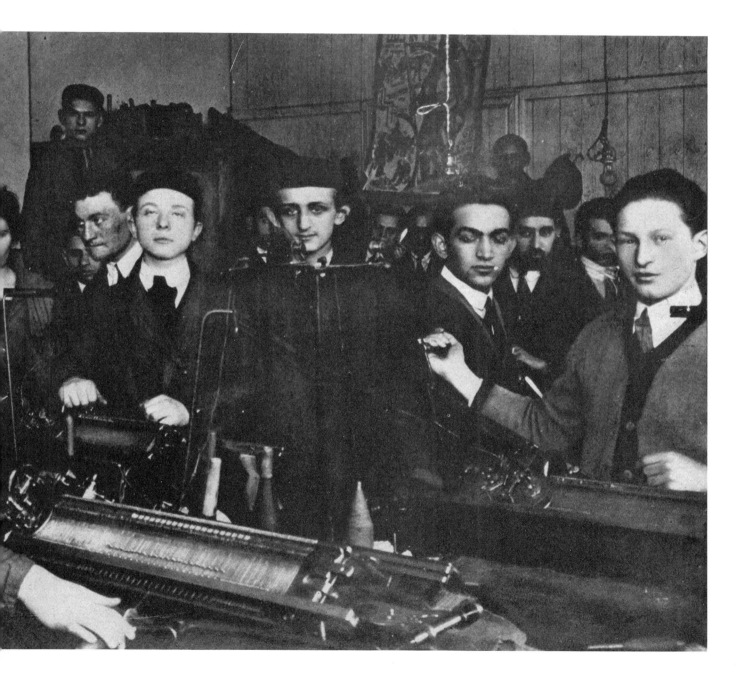

WORK

According to popular belief, the majority of the shtetl's inhabitants were *luft-menschen,* people who made their living out of thin air. Nothing is further from the truth. The Jews knew very well the meaning of the harsh Biblical phrase "In the sweat of thy brow shalt thou eat bread." The shtetl's inhabitants were engaged in a hard struggle for their daily living—made harder by the restrictions and discriminations imposed by their non-Jewish rulers.

Shtetl Jews could be found in all areas of human activity—in wholesale trade as well as in small business, in manual work, and in all sorts of crafts. There were also specific shtetl occupations such as matchmaker, circumciser, matzoh bakers, and "manufacturer" of fringed garments— strange occupations which grew from the uniqueness of Jewish life.

The purpose of work was to make a living; but for the majority of shtetl dwellers making a living was not in any way the most important purpose of life.

Opposite: A milkman carrying pails.

Above: Chaim the boatman, who transported passengers across the Vistula River; he appears as a character in one of Sholem Asch's books. Opposite top: A Jewish merchant selling farm supplies to a Lithuanian peasant woman. Opposite bottom: A water carrier.

120

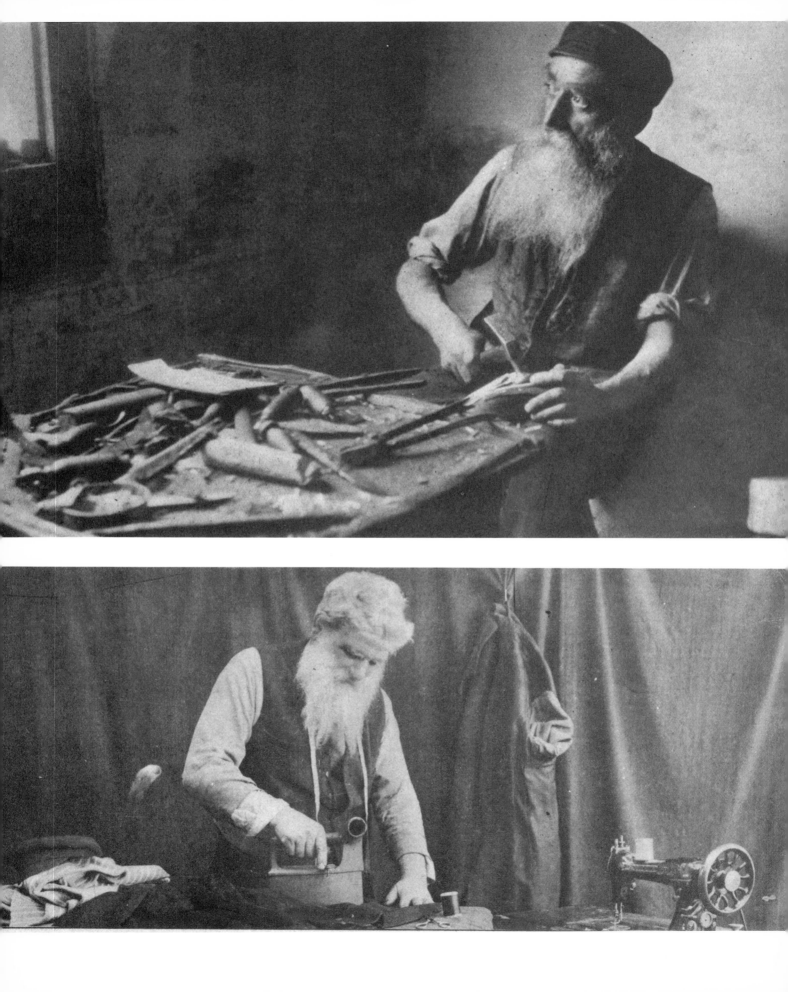

Above: A glazier carrying glass along a street. Opposite top: A bootmaker.
Opposite bottom: A tailor.

Above: This man walked around the streets of Vilna offering to mend chairs. Opposite: A *cheder* teacher in Biala, Poland.

A family of Jewish smiths—a father and his three sons in Zhelechow, Poland.

Opposite: A baker selling his wares in a Galician market; his cart is made of woven straw. Above: Preparing matzohs for Passover. Left: A bagel peddler.

129

Above: Jewish wheat merchants. Opposite: A matchmaker in Kovno, Lithuania, inspecting his list of clients to find a prospect for this young man.

Above: A father and son, both peddlers of old clothes in Warsaw.
Opposite: Three elderly rag dealers.

Above: A Jewish farmer, still at work at the age of eighty-six. Opposite: A Polish peasant selling his cow to a Jewish dealer.

135

Opposite top: An open-air butcher shop. Opposite below: Four ritual slaughterers displaying their work tools. Right: A kosher butcher posed in front of his chopping block.

Making a living from the dead. Above:
A psalm sayer in the old shul of Vilna.
Opposite: Professional wailers at the
cemetery of Vilna. Right: A man who
made a living by collecting money for
intoning the prayer for the dead for
those visiting the graves of their
relatives in Warsaw.

A group of Jewish porters, members of the Porters' Union in Kutno, Poland.

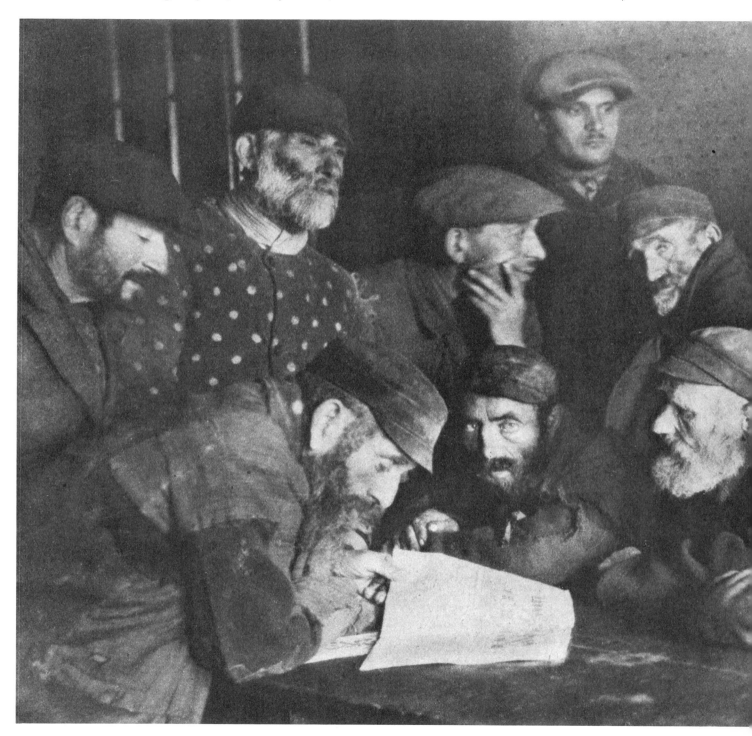

Opposite top: Jewish lumber workers in Pinsk. Opposite bottom: Jewish loggers. Below: An elderly wood cutter splitting kindling.

Below: A Jewish saddle maker. Right: A family of water carriers in Opatow, Poland. Opposite bottom: A Jewish peddler collecting newly shorn wool in the Carpathian mountains.

146

Opposite: Shingle makers at work in their open air shop.
Below: A woman plucking feathers, used for stuffing
pillows and eiderdowns.

Above: An organ grinder and his parrot at the summer resort in Falenica, Poland; for a fee he gave out little cards with fortunes written on them. Opposite top: A roofer at work. Right: Teachers and pupils at a trade school in Minsk, Russia, at the end of the last century; the school principal is at the center.

149

Above: A chicken dealer. Opposite: A group of Jewish actors in Warsaw studying the theater pages of *The Jewish Daily Forward* of New York. Many of them would eventually appear in the flourishing Yiddish theaters on New York's Second Avenue.

151

RELIGION

Religion in the shtetl was not simply a system of beliefs
and rituals, it was a style of life that enveloped all aspects of
individual and collective behavior, a discipline which
functioned twenty-four hours a day. It shaped one's reality
and dreams, one's attitude toward life and death, toward
joys and sorrow. It formed man's relationship to his fellow
man, to animals, and to nature. It dictated the kind of food
to be consumed, the style and color of clothes to be worn;
it permeated every stage of education, language, culture,
and folklore.

It was as impossible for an inhabitant of a shtetl to
leave the compounds of religion as it would be to get out
of one's skin. Religion was not only a way of life, it
was life itself.

Opposite: A man carrying a *lulav* and *ethrog* (palm branch and citron)
in preparation for the celebration of the festival of Succoth.

154

Opposite: The beadle of the Lublin shul lights the candles on the eve of Sabbath.
Below: The old synagogue of Shargrod.

Clockwise, from right: The Holy Ark in Wyszogrod; interior of the old shul in Lublin; the 800-year-old shul of Zabludów, near Bialystok; the Great Shul of Ostrowiec; the pulpit in Konin.

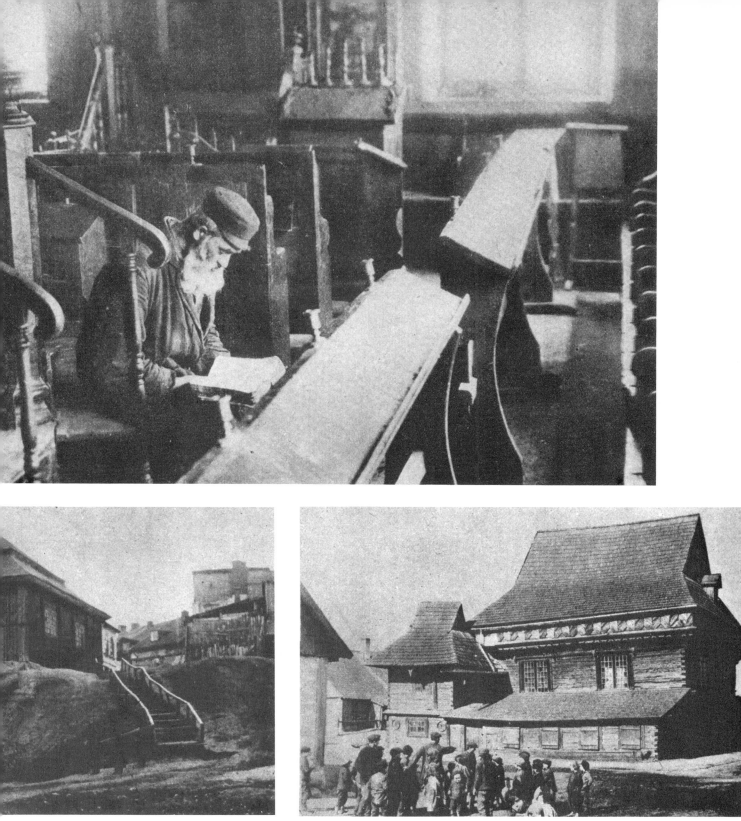

Above: Yeshivah boys of Warsaw studying the Talmud. Opposite: Young yeshivah students in Lipsk, Poland.

Right: Making the parchment upon which the Torah will be written. Opposite top: Scribes examining a copy of the Torah for accuracy. Opposite bottom: A scribe wears a prayer shawl and phylacteries while making a copy of the Torah.

Above: The curtain for the Holy Ark and the mantle covering the Torah scroll (on the left) were embroidered by the girls of a Jewish school for industrial arts. Opposite top: Jews of Pinsk risked their lives in order to save the Torahs when a fire broke out in their ancient synagogue. Opposite bottom: The synagogue from which the scrolls were saved, after the fire.

Above: Studying the Talmud in one of the old synagogues in Vilna.
Opposite: A peddler selling prayer books and ritual articles.

Above: Members of the Butchers' Synagogue in Slonim, Poland. Opposite: Returning home after services. Right: A beadle burning leavened bread for the inhabitants of his shtetl on the eve of Passover.

Jews reciting psalms in the shul of Luck, in the Ukraine.

SECULARIZATION

For hundreds of years the shtetl was a fortress against the influences of the outside world. Except for minor nuances, the essentials of its life style remained unchanged. Only at the turn of the last century did the "fingers of time" make major breaks in the shtetl's immunity, and the process of secularization began.

Orthodox Jews regarded secularization with suspicion—particularly the secularization of schools and the emergence of political movements. They believed that any infiltration of new learning might bring about the destruction of the shtetl's way of life. In truth, however, though secularization affected many aspects of behavior, it brought modifications only to the outer shell of shtetl life. Usually the shtetl's basic ideology remained unchanged.

Opposite: A group of Jewish political prisoners on their way to Siberian exile for their part in the 1905 revolution.

Clockwise, from opposite top: a Jewish soldier in the Austrian army; a dandy-fied *maskil* (follower of the *Enlightenment* movement); the daughter of a rabbi, who eloped to Palestine with her lover against her parents' wishes; a group of Jewish soldiers, members of a cavalry regiment in tsarist Russia in 1902.

Clockwise, from top left: Bundists at work in a factory; two Jewish members of the Polish Senate; a group of young Bundists, photographed in 1905, the year of the first Russian Revolution; leaders of a Jewish workers union in Minsk in 1899.

Left: A group of young Pinsk Jews organized in self-defense against pogrom bands. Opposite bottom: A group of Jewish emigrants at the railway station of Danzig. Destination: America. Below: Two blacksmith brothers from Lithuania; it was a sign of the times that one of them has shaved off his beard.

Opposite: These three young women were chosen as the winners in a beauty contest for the title of "Miss Judea." Clockwise from left: Zofia Oldak, "Miss Judea," and Janina Wilczer and Maria Lobzowska, the two runners-up; all three have Polish rather than Yiddish first names. Below: A girl helps her friend put on lipstick. Before secularization beauty contests and cosmetics were unheard of in the shtetl.

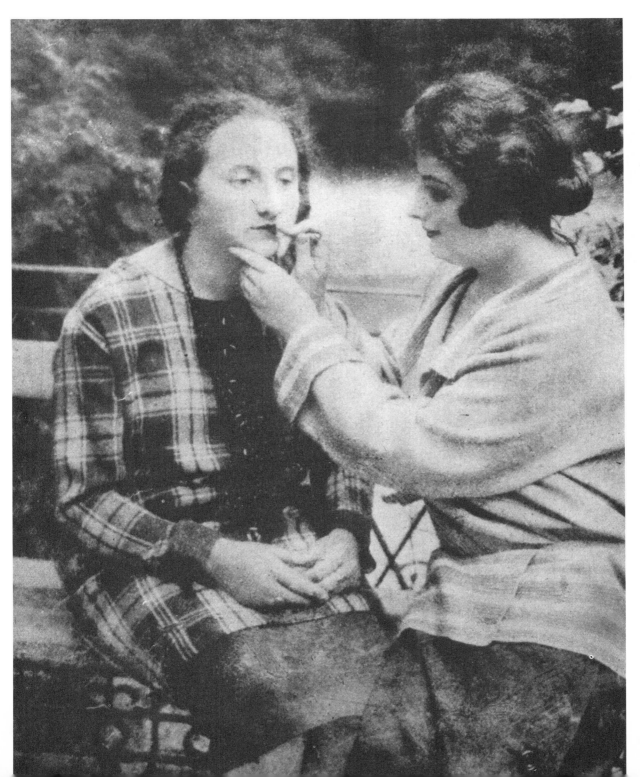

A FAMILY ALBUM

The great majority of the Jews in the United States, as well as in the other English-speaking countries and Latin America, originally came from the little towns in Eastern Europe. Many American homes may still preserve old, leather-bound albums containing half-faded photos of men with strange whiskers, women wearing unusual crown pieces on their heads, and children dressed in the most fantastic attire.

The further removed the photos are from us in time, the more abstract and legendary become the faces on these fading portraits. It is in this sense that the photos on the following pages now scarcely relate to any particular family; they represent the common ancestors of the multitude of Western Jews—all those who trace their origin to the world of the shtetl.

Opposite: A young Jewish family from Volhynia.

Below: An old man studying the Talmud. Opposite: The little son of a ritual slaughterer from Kurczew, Poland, studying the Bible.

Clockwise, from top right: A
cantor and his wife; a family of
Jewish peasants with their cow
and horse; a seven-year-old boy
named Hirsch Greenblat, sent
all by himself from Kielce,
Poland, to his relatives in
America; a schoolteacher from
a shtetl near Minsk, with his
wife and daughter; an elderly
man and his bedridden wife.

185

186

Above: A yeshivah boy of Piaseczno, Poland.
Opposite: A venerable Jew of Nowogrodek, Poland.

Opposite: A ninety-year-old man of Laskirow. Right: G. Miranski, the chief of the Jewish volunteer firemen in Minsk. Below: Elchanon Katz, the assistant rabbi of Volkovysk, Poland, surrounded by members of his family.

Above: A shoemaker at work, with his family in the background.
Opposite: A Jewish couple with thirteen children.

Left: Three young men standing before the office of the American Consulate in Warsaw, waiting for their visas. Below: A set of triplets, thirteen-year-old musical sisters of Warsaw. Opposite: A typical Galician Jewish family.

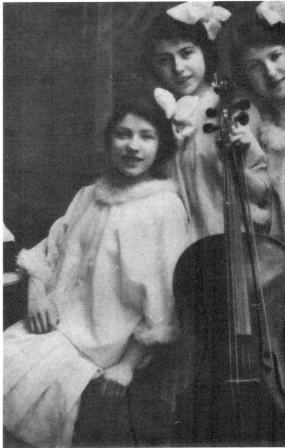

Above: Two orthodox dandies.
Opposite: Three brothers.

Above, top: Men in a Jewish old-age home in Vilna. Above bottom: Women in the Vilna home for the aged—the oldest is 113 years old. Opposite: An elderly citizen of Wyszkow, Poland.

Left: A family group. Above: A man named Berel Diment of Radzyn, Poland, with his granddaughter.

Above: A man who migrated to America and returned on a visit to the old country, photographed with his parents. Left: The meagre repast of a Jewish family from Kosow, Poland.

202

Right: Reb Isak Jakow Reines, who taught Hebrew to the great Russian writer Leo Tolstoy. Below: A famous scholar, Rebbe Itzhak Sosnes, who was awarded a decoration for his learning by Tsar Alexander II. Opposite: A wedding picture—two bridegrooms and their brides.

204

Opposite top: A water carrier. Opposite bottom: A shoemaker. Below: A Jewish family named Cerny from the Ukraine. The young man in the second row was later killed in a pogrom.

Below: A man teaching his grandson the alphabet while the child's grand-mother looks on. Opposite: A beadle photographed standing outside a *Succah*.

208

Above: Two fashionable sisters of Warsaw at the turn of the century. Left: A yeshivah student. Opposite top: Two pictures of the same man, Chaim Velvel Warshawskyk—bearded in Poland and clean-shaven after he emigrated to the United States. Opposite bottom: A typical Galician family: Mordechai Meyer, his wife, and two sons.

209

Migrants, Jewish and non-Jewish, with their luggage, in Danzig en route to America.